DARWIN'S MICROSCOPE

Kelley Swain is a poet, novelist, and critic specialising in medical and health humanities and natural history. Her first novel, *Double the Stars*, and her second poetry collection, *Atlantic*, were both published in 2014 by Cinnamon Press. Her verse drama, *Opera di Cera*, was published by Valley Press in 2014. *The Naked Muse*, a memoir about working as an artists' model, was published by Valley Press in 2016. She lives on a farm in rural Oxfordshire, and is working on her second novel.

by the same author, available from Valley Press

OPERA DI CERA
THE NAKED MUSE

Darwin's Microscope

Kelley Swain

Valley Press

First published in 2009 by Flambard Press

This second edition first published in 2019 by Valley Press
Woodend, The Crescent, Scarborough, YO11 2PW
www.valleypressuk.com

Second edition, first printing (October 2019)

ISBN 978-1-912436-26-2
Cat. no. VP0146

Copyright © Kelley Swain 2009, 2019

The right of Kelley Swain to be identified as the
author of this work has been asserted in accordance with
the Copyright, Designs and Patents Act 1988.

All rights reserved. No part of this publication may be
reproduced, stored in or introduced into a retrieval system,
or transmitted in any form, by any means (electronic,
mechanical, photocopying, recording or otherwise) without
prior written permission from the rights holders.

A CIP record for this book is available from the British Library.

Cover illustration by Katherine Child.
Text design by Jamie McGarry.

Printed and bound in Great Britain by
Imprint Digital, Upton Pyne, Exeter.

Contents

Introduction 7

I. VESTIGES

Shadows in Chalk 19
Darwin's Letter 20
Deprived of its Medium 21
Fossil Memories 22
Down, Bromley 24

II. VOYAGE

Morning Watch 27
Ship's Naturalist 28
Cetacean Introduction 29
New Hand on Deck 31
Glacier Blue 32
Loss of a Whale 33
Submersible Captain 35
Bones 37
The Unsettling of Dunes 38
Tectonic Motion 39
Bird Island, Baja 41
Reverse Cartography 42
Eulogy for a Cephalopod 43
Towards Perfection 46

III. ORIGINS

What the Toad Said 49
In the Lab 50
Illumination of an Empty Room 59
A Smoke at Dusk 61
The Smells of Good Death and Bad Death 62

A Fall Evening   64
Lovely Mollusk   65
Feeding the Corn Snake   66
The Ninth Commandment   67
Thermodynamics of Immortality   68

IV. DESCENT

Pure Admiration   71
Mating of the Silkworm Moth   72
The Lake District   73
Plumed Magician   74
Fallen Armor   76
The Katydid Chorus   79
Monarch Sunset   80
Spherical Motion   81

V. MOULT

Of Caddisflies and Kings   85
Chicken as time-piece   86
Persephone   87
Ab ovo   88
Pasture, 7am   89
Criatura   90
From the Storm   91
How Myth Works   92
Kingfisher   93
Terra nullis   94
On East Beach   95
Harvest   96
Airing   97
Fox Not Crow   98
Refrain   102

Endnotes   104
Acknowledgements   105

Introduction

"a poet in a room full of scientists", or Writing from a Liminal Space

The publication of the tenth-anniversary edition of Kelley Swain's *Darwin's Microscope* is to be celebrated. And not only because the physical book is made available again – no small achievement in these digital times – but because it gives us the opportunity to revisit the poet's debut collection in the context of international debates on the current geological era, the Anthropocene, characterised by overwhelming evidence on climate change and the negative impact of human activity on the Earth. American biologist Edward O. Wilson prefers to call this new epoch the Age of Loneliness, poetic terminology indeed to intimate the progressive disappearance of ecosystems and the subsequent solitude humans will be doomed to if the damage to our planet continues. With protests against climate change escalating, and demonstrations of ecological grief taking place worldwide, there is now an urgency to search for reciprocal ways of relating to our environment. *Darwin's Microscope* definitely contributes to the search. And it does so with a kind, though firm, poetic stance.

This is a book informed by the natural world and the natural sciences, as evidenced by its title, which does not refer to a specific poem but rather gives unity to the entire collection. The nineteenth-century English naturalist Charles Darwin and his celebrated work *On the Origin of Species* act as the sustained background reference for the poet's microscopic look at her surroundings. However, Swain's observations of the myriad organisms in the natural world – insects, reptiles, mammals, molluscs – do not aspire to produce supposedly objective knowledge on the origins of life but instead pose questions – and also find answers – of deep emotional significance that complement, but are not incompatible with, scientific research.

In the first section – *Vestiges* – the poet draws attention to the material aspects of life and inscribes both the signifying power of matter and its quality of endurance in the face of human finitude: as in the sediments "of a hundred thousand years" embedded in the White Cliffs of Dover and perceived as immortal in "Shadows in Chalk"; as in "Darwin's Letter", based on the correspondence that the eminent scientist sent to J. E. Todd asking for seeds and which is still preserved in the archives of the University of Kansas; and as in "Fossil Memories", where the poetic persona wonders what is left of Darwin "when two hundred years have passed" and concluding: "little but a fossil of a man". All through this opening section there is the underlying sense that matter matters, that it preserves some truth, and, as such, that it takes the place that John Keats had reserved for art in his "Ode on a Grecian Urn". In the face of human mortality and immanence, the romantic poet found comfort in the permanence of the eponymous urn, where the two lovers – though never consummating their kiss – will forever be suspended in that pre-climatic moment of expectation that precedes the touching of their lips. In *Vestiges* both the beauty that is truth and the truth that is beauty lie in the material traces that outlive us.

Informed by water, the second section – *Voyage* – is reminiscent of the five-year journey Darwin undertook aboard H. M. S. Beagle to collect fossils and to observe marine invertebrates. It is also an Odyssey of sorts where the "strange mist that settled on the ship" ("Morning Watch") and the occasional quest narrative – "for months our ship sailed / through clear waters" ("Ship's Naturalist") – create an atmosphere of mystery and prepare the reader for adventure. However, here, the expeditions previously reserved for warrior-heroes and male scientists are experienced by a poetic I in search of wisdom. The poems in this section leave no room for human exceptionality and instead emphasise our vulnerability: confronted with a whale, "you suddenly feel small", admits our particular naturalist, "when the breath breaks / the surface / next to you / rocking your boat" ("Cetacean Introduction"); and with respect to the magnificent ocean, she acknowledges her own physical and existential proportions – "I am not even a speck / in this deadly element" ("New Hand on Deck"). The veneration of the material traces of life that we saw in *Vestiges* is sustained in *Voyage*, becoming particularly evident in "Submersible Captain", a poem with echoes of Adrienne Rich's "Diving into the Wreck". In the latter text, the female protagonist descends into the ocean to save what had been lost and forgotten, symbolised by that famous "book of myths / in which / our names do not appear". The quest of Rich's heroine was to rescue from oblivion women's stories and genealogies. In a similar vein, in Swain's text the mission of the poetic persona is to search for a submarine, an esteemed "relic of war". But the journey takes an unexpected turn when she encounters, instead, the bones of a whale, "a different relic / on the uneven floor". In spite of the indifferent darkness, the remains of the big mammal are honoured through an improvised burial ritual: "I am the first, the only, / to kneel at this grave".

Origins, the third section of *Darwin's Microscope*, functions as a poetic visit to a museum of natural history. Various organisms, deprived of life, are displayed in cases and jars for students, researchers and general visitors alike. These poems offer detailed descriptions of the physical characteristics of gastropods, mammals, reptiles, birds and insects, the specific names of their body parts becoming in the process poetic material. Walking the museum in the company of the poet we find ourselves in the midst of an uncomfortable paradox: while there is the sustained belief that scientific enquiry is necessary in the pursuit of knowledge, we are also tormented by the dehumanisation and fragmentation of non-human bodies, here used as the passive objects of that same scientific research. In "Arthropoda", for instance, the poet wonders what stories lie hidden behind each of the dried insects on display – "Did this cicada / mate before it died?" – and in "Reptilia" she is saddened by the skeleton of a sea turtle, imprisoned in a jar, but to which her imagination adds "flesh and colour / until it swims in Caribbean waters". She is a poet amongst scientists, the odd woman out. And that makes all the difference.

All these reflections culminate in *Descent*, the section that closed the original edition of this full-of-wonder collection. The species divide that privileges humans above the rest of living organisms is denounced once again in poems that underline the smallness and the creatureliness of men and women. The human gaze, that instrument that separates subjects from objects, loses its traditional power in "Plumed Magician": "We think we spy / through binocular / lenses", explains the poetic voice, but the falcon that is being looked at ignores the human observers and disappears. After succumbing to the magnificence of the natural world, the poet articulates a final balance in "Spherical Motion", the equilibrium found in a world that humans belong to, rather than dominate.

Now, ten years after its first publication, *Darwin's Microscope* is still relevant. Still urgent. Now, as then, Swain's poetic reflections feel valid. And they are as fresh. Readers familiar with the original book will notice, though, that a final section, *Moult*, has been added. In the new poems the natural world is still the main source of knowledge, but the timid observations of the earlier poetic voice have become confident conclusions proven by experience. In the process of growth some animals shed their skins or shells, what is known as moulting. Swain's appropriation of this generative cycle is indicative of a new departure – be it personal or artistic – but it also refers to her understanding of humans as animals inserted in the natural order or, as Mary Oliver would put it, that have their "place / in the family of things".

In *Moult* non-humans become the key to understanding and to interpreting what we humans call reality. And so, a new love – the "we" that runs through "Of Caddisflies and Kings" – merges with the "bursting / into a new element, a new relationship / to gravity" of the eponymous insects that transform themselves from aquatic larvae into terrestrial adults; in "Chicken as time-piece", man-made instruments to measure time and space are presented as artificial, unnecessary even, in the business of farm life: the cyanometer may determine the degree of blueness in the sky but in the end it is the hens who "keep the time" while their human owners must simply listen. In line with the earlier poems, *Moult* displays Swain's interest in water. Human history has traditionally suffered from what John R. Gillis has called "terracentricity", i.e., our inability to consider place as anything but land. However,

Swain's rivers, seas, oceans and beaches, across Europe as well as in her native Rhode Island, are full of life, stories and history. The sea resists being treated as an instrument purely for leisure – "Today is not for swimming", says the poetic persona in "From the Storm" – and instead its "foaming tentacles" have the power to transgress "the margins / we have invented for them". Affects and emotions are also interpreted from a non-human perspective in "How Myth Works", one of the most moving poems in the collection. The mythical figure of the Gryphon – part lion, part eagle – who mated for life, is compared to the poet's mother, a widow for whom "to remain a survivor might mean / remaining unrecovered". The poem ultimately questions the cultural construction of pain and relies, instead, on our potential for healing.

Kelley Swain is an inhabitant of liminal spaces. In my classes at university, I invariably define liminality as the gap in between two worlds, or two languages, or to differentiated realms of existence. If you live in a liminal space, you can easily feel excluded from the normative systems that regulate belonging and identity (not necessarily a bad thing); but, as an in-betweener, you are also in a vantage point where you can experience two worlds at the same time, in other words, you are inhabiting the space where magic happens. When reading *Darwin's Microscope* we are not completely sure of our bearings. After all, we have been schooled in the radical separation of the so-called two cultures – the sciences and the humanities – and feeling we are navigating both from within a small poem-boat can be puzzling, disorienting. Such a journey may require the unlearning of what we believed was solid factual information. An expedition to the unexplored routes of liminality is always an adventurous quest. But, in spite of all the challenges and destabilising uncertainties, who wouldn't like to visit the space where magic happens?

Luz Mar González-Arias
Profesora Titular de Filología Inglesa
Senior Lecturer in English and Irish Studies
Universidad de Oviedo, Spain

Ex omnia conchis

(all from shells)

'Sweet is the lore which Nature brings;
Our meddling intellect
Mis-shapes the beauteous forms of things:
We murder to dissect.'

Wordsworth

1. Vestiges

Shadows in Chalk

at the White Cliffs of Dover

Silken outlines on a wall with scars and scrapes,
crystallized and hidden places.

Shadows leaning hard against a white cliff face
above a channel, splitting continents.

Silhouettes in sediment, of a hundred thousand years,
sea creatures crushed to dust, soaked with rain and blood.

Shapes unchanging only while the sun remains,
immortalized in chalk, lines we scrape and wipe away.

Darwin's Letter

Yellow-blossomed partridge-pea,
hard-thorned buffalo bur:

asking for these seeds
with his humble Victorian air,

Charles Darwin wrote a letter.
He had a wish to *experimentise:*

*I have read with unusual interest
your very interesting paper…*

*on the flowers of <u>Solanum rostratum</u>…
if you would send me some seeds…*

Though the letter reached its mark,
nine days later, Darwin died.

Deprived of its Medium

Hope is the thing with feathers
Bird in a bell jar
That perches in the soul,
suffocating –
and sings the tune without the words,
proves the ether
and never stops at all
runs out.

Fossil Memories

...or, what is left of Darwin.

What is left of a man
when two hundred years have passed,
his cousins distantly pleased
with their thin-running blood,
his face on a banknote,

his home a museum
where ten children played, where he fell ill
and roused himself to walks and work countless times,
where he loved his family but lost his faith,
where he hesitated and wondered and was spooked
into writing a book which changed our future
as well as our past.

See him wrapped in cold towels
shaking with fever, or turning from his daughter's
death-bed, knowing his wife's God
would be her only solace,
or turning from his son's death-bed,
never saying aloud how nature had selected against
this loved but deficient boy.

See him hunched at a wooden table,
one hundred barnacles systematically aligned,
his touchy stomach the worse for the alcohol-preservative smell,
his eyes squinted towards the creatures he came to hate.

Weathering of time,
rust of human memory,
snowflakes of a glacier,
pebbles of a mountain,
fist-sized rock of a whale's baleen,
little but a fossil of a man.

Down, Bromley

Black-eyed sheep
graze a February-flooded field.
Wood-pigeon, fat, suspended,
and red-breast singing –
singing over cold February stone.
Bright sharp sun in a blue sky
over couples of mallards –
sleek-headed sapphire Drake
or emerald – she chooses.
Glistening mud and green,
trying, hopeful,
in the certain spring.
Clumped cattails, a dredged canal –
and a church spire, always, distant.

II. Voyage

Morning Watch

As a hard-boiled sun
cracked the horizon near
arid Patagonia,
a strange mist settled on the ship.

Every drop of frosted glass lived,
each delicate dancing snowflake
a just-hatched spider,
their thousand bodies a web
of twinkling dew upon the deck.

One by one, the translucent drops
lifted ethereal lassos
to the wind, whose breath
ballooned them to parachute-flight
onto the sea, evaporating
the mist as silently as it had come.

Ship's Naturalist

It was futile, I decided,
to look for red tides.

The animalcules making them up
come and go with the currents:

for months our ship sailed
through clear waters.

One morning, roused by shouts
from the crew, I hurried on deck

to see red water surrounding us,
stretching as far as I could see,

grainy, orangey-red,
a swathe of rust-water.

The surface was broken
by buoyant bodies of dead fish;

seabirds wheeled overhead,
screaming, diving after them.

I scooped a jar of water,
held it, my hands trembling

with excitement, the water
trembling with life.

A droplet under my microscope
quivered with broken ruby snowflakes.

The next morning the sea was clear,
as if the red tide had never been.

Cetacean Introduction

The whale does not
exist to you,
in your small boat
with the water
an obsidian dance floor
for the birds you watch,
with the water
unbroken by creatures
you do not imagine
underneath,
        does not
exist to you,
in your orange life-vest,
with notebook close-
gripped and binoculars
settled for looking
to the skies,
        does not
exist to you
as the wind tugs
your hair, combing
it with salt and low-tide smell
from the mountains of shells
piled on the beach upwind.

So when the water changes,
when the birds yell
and lift off,
when you suddenly feel
small,
when the breath breaks
the surface
next to you

rocking your boat,
when you grip your
life-vest,
when your binoculars
fall and you stare
at the grey mountain
rising from the sea,
which rolls and rolls,
a barnacled stage,
marked and polished
and marked –

After the back thins
and rolls away
into a wide fin
with a mountain range
along its edge,
after it slips
below the gloss
sending ripples outward
to slide under your small boat,
after the birds return
and settle,
after puffs of wind
sweep the smooth
glassy footprint away,
after you loosen
your grip on the life-vest
and your boat stops
rocking,

you turn your gaze down

to look past
the obsidian glaze.

New Hand on Deck

Legs wobble,
stomach turns

like this cork
I bob on in the sea.

Ocean? It means awe.
Dread.

I am not even a speck
in this deadly element.

Why did I join the crew
of this damnable vessel?

They laugh as I puke
shellfish over the port side,

tell me I will
"find my sea legs soon."

But fins, flippers,
not legs,

are what I need.
I will not "find" them.

Glacier Blue

The glacier takes sun into itself.

Gathers the colors – red, orange, yellow, green –
collecting them into cold compression.

Thousands of years of ice compacting, squeezing out air –
it can collect the sun, breathlessly suck in the colors –
but one escapes.

Blue. glacier blue –
not blue like the sky or Caribbean seas,
not like the robin's egg or the silk iris petal –

glacier blue.

Quicker than red, orange, yellow, green –
these colors fall into the glacier and cannot turn back –

glacier blue shivers away in time to escape –

to glow from the ice
so it is the only color we see.

Loss of a Whale

The giant carcass sinks
into the abyss, taking
barnacles on its belly,
suckerfish on its side,
tons of blubber, gallons of oil,
racks of baleen to fossilize
into small black rocks;
taking wails, clicks, echoes,
that will sound no more
as the body sinks past the reach
of sunlight into the crushing dark,
past schools of porpoise,
past eight-legged giants, small beside it;
water rushes past the curving fluke,
fanned out, bending up
in a final flip; streams of bubbles
float to the surface, glimmer and pop
thousands of feet above, a chain
linking whitecaps to the deep fathoms.

First the giant sinks past nothing,
last breath pouring out,
pressure bending in a body
which has never traveled so deep;
now pulls heavily past wrecks
of humanity; great broken ships,
splintered masts,
the arching figurehead
of a lady's bust,
hair and breasts covered
with green slime,
her companions empty skulls,

skittering silent creatures,
her blind eyes watching the carcass
float down in the pitch,
lit only by phosphorescent pulses
of pigment-less life,
every pulse of the creatures
revealing organs built to withstand
the smothering dark, the sea floor.

The whale slowly touches,
delicately crushes rock,
blind glowing creatures,
comes to rest
where undersea vents
provide an oasis
of nutrient heat in the freezing dark,
bubbling up red life
where no sunlight
is needed or ever seen;
the body stretches, meters long,
into the dark, while hagfish,
ancient slimy creatures
wriggling along the ocean floor,
feed solely on whale remains.

Submersible Captain

A small metal
placenta,

protecting me from all
my body cannot withstand:

darkness, water pressure,
lack of oxygen.

Remote gears whirr, buzz;
I descend, slowly.

Powerful lamp a spark
in the Black Forest,

the beam reaches –
I search for the wreck,

relic of war,
submarine,

find a different relic
on the uneven floor.

Whale bones glint
into view;

Not white, no sun
to bleach them,

great grey ribs
bend into darkness.

The vessel settles
into mechanical twilight.

I am the first, the only,
to kneel at this grave.

Bones

Bones   in the rock
            in the ice
            in the dirt
            in the water.

An island made of bones.

A planet made of bones,
bones of ancestors
fallen   from wars,
            from predators
            from disease,

fallen
            from never having stood.

Bones sinking
            into mud
            into earth
            into lava
            into sea floor,

bones compressed
            to chalk
            to coal

            which we use to heat our bones.

The Unsettling of Dunes

First we run our feet through silken sediment,
undulating dunes plucked particle
after particle by fingers of wind.

Then we feel the muffled crunch
of calcium carbonate layers beneath
from chalk of ivory sand dollar,
crumpled keel of pelican, dust of reptile,
scale of fish, shell of oyster,
to sift through our fingers, and *sedimentum.*

Ooids compress with the weight of sand,
of in-seeping water,
laminae after laminae coming to rest
one on another until they fuse,
and coquina along the shore
hold mosaic shells until waves abrade
and they crumble, *sedimentum,*
to be curled from beach to sea,
to be sifted, floated, carried,
to be filtered by fish, pelicans, oysters,
sand dollars, and again,
sedimentum.

Tectonic Motion

We chart it, draw it,
connect its dots,
measure, compile,
assess, organize.

We embrace it, deny it,
think nothing of it, but it is there,

churning itself through rain,
heat, earthquakes, volcanoes;
through tectonic plates grinding
almost too slow to measure;
through ghosts of icebergs
leaving boulders and grooves behind.

Slow time. Not our time.

We see drastic changes wrought by
time slower than we will ever comprehend,
slower than all the generations of our families,
slower than the time before our ancestors
had legs, or were naked, or stood.

Time slower than before anything lived on land,
time slower than before anything lived.

It is neither there for us,
nor against us. It is there.

It will be there long after charts, diagrams,
pictures, specimens, books have evaporated
to dust, disappearing with the wind, ground back
into the great mortar of molecules of Earth,
and no one will exist to call it "Earth."

There will be no one to remember,
no one to forget, no one watching,
and it will still carry on.

Bird Island, Baja

Thrust of foot, flush of feather –
I hold my breath; they walk on water.

Cormorant, pelican, a dark stampede
of hollow bones rattles around me.
An acrid beach, living sand
where black stains white,
spills to bay. The moving island, lifting.
Necks strain against gravity.

Hundreds of wings pump a heartbeat on water.

I am an eye in this storm, this rushing
whispering roar of foot and feather.

Reverse Cartography

Those tiny worms in sea mud
are your truly ancient ancestors,
and is it bad?

They are before bad, good, gross;
before Adam and Eve,
before legs, brains, eyes.

Before feeling,
before thinking,
before words,
before six thousand years ago,

before alive things left the seas,
before alive things returned to the seas,
before alive things left the seas again.

The magnet of north switches with south,
continents crash, pull apart,
ice coats, melts, re-coats land,
tides rise, fall, rise again,
heat bubbles from inside,

and the churning pressure-cooker
outside the crust, the most animated
of inanimate forces, determines what persists
on a map only chartable in reverse.

Eulogy for a Cephalopod

1.

Dark myth,
Giant Terror –
suckers, tearing arms,
razor beak:
The Kraken pulls ships
to the crushing Deep.

As a child I stand tiptoe,
nose pressed to cool glass
filled with twilight water,
peering into blue depths,
searching for The Monster.

It does not appear.

II.

Years later, peering again
through glass into dim blue,
I see the octopus in full bloom.

The billowing parachute
breathes water;
see-through skin
and glass-kissing suckers
putty-stretch in every direction,
whisk the water, stirring
a whirlpool of pigment-stained flesh
which dances over rock and plant,
rusty orange and brown
in the twilight water.

The eye –
yellow, round, large,
sees *me*.

III.

The surf is too heavy
to wade deeper than our feet,
but sand-coated relics
cross-stitch the high tide line.

We peer, and wonder:
"What is it?"
"An octopus."
"Is it dead?"
"Don't touch it."

Noodle-tangled arms,
plum-sized head.
It is round, translucent,
and as we crouch
the center swirls
and pulses with blue.

"It's alive."

I take an abalone shell
from my pile
of beach-combed treasures,
gently scoop the octopus
so it rests
for a moment
in the iridescent moon.

Towards Perfection

Long, slow, unplanned precision:
deceptive perfection, this spiny scallop,
glossy purple-and-white,
the whorl incrementally widening
with each smooth ridge.

Read a simple fortune
in its parallel-lined palm:
the lifeline is the outer edge,
where the throwing over
of each new layer ceased.

Protection grown, accident
enhancing standard armor.
Brittle-plated fish-defying bivalve,
sharply outstretching
vaulted pink-and-brown cousins.

Invaded by a symmetrical hole
drilled precisely beside the spines
where another mollusk reached in,
dissolving the soft flesh,
or a small octopus embraced the shell,
using its only sharp part –
its beak – to scrape persistently,
grinding each layer away, stretching in
a thin arm, grasping the flesh,
leaving the shell hollow,
the unplanned sculpture drifting,
polished by tongues of waves.

III. Origins

What the Toad Said

The botanist
said there was no toad
in the greenhouse,
but we had heard him
belching through
the fog and dew
of the locked room
where mist whispered
through heavy air
onto ginko,
liverwort,
Queen Anne's lace,
onto the far wall of rock
covered with hanging ferns,
soft moss, and mold,
the room where flecks of dust
transmuted into prisms
as they drifted
into creamy sunlight
streaking through pollen-
dusted windows,
the room where we closed the door
to breathe
the reciprocal breath
of *flora, flora, everywhere.*

In the Lab

1. Survey

Embryos of chicken and pig,
necks folded at obtuse angles,
yellow in jars. Humming
vent swallows fumes; cool
musk permeates, mixes
with mothball, formalin, dust.

Jaws, scales, fur, and feathers,
all stiffened. Iridescent shingles
on purple *Lepidoptera*.
Trilobite fossils from Utah,
thumbnail-sized.

Parrot, eagle, old penguin
crusty with dandruff.
Wood duck wire-stiffened
into permanent flight.
Empty, peeling box-tortoise shell.
Snakes spiraled into glass
with faded labels, withered egg-cases.
Eyeless snapping turtles,
rusty-pink, rotting, stuffed, tagged,
boxed, jarred, examined.

11. Gastropoda

Endangered Queen: pale conch,
dethroned, sitting heavy on a shelf.
Slow-stretching foot, snail-creature,
leaked this crown into hard existence
under crush of salt water.

Linear development? Tiny spiral at first,
whorling continuously outward, around.

III. Echinodermata

Tangled woven basket-star
lashed across the ocean floor,
arms of rope now dried
brittle and hard.

Sand dollars, in childhood,
were pirate gold,
now they are animals
related to sea urchins:
brittle shell, five-lobed stamp
filtering microscopic food:
dried in boxes, broken
filters leak sand.

IV. ARTHROPODA

Plastic dish, dried insects:
a huge, swept-off
window ledge.
Sharp, spiny, mean, brittle wings,
trick-of-my-eye movements –
they *are* dead –
as I turn the dish.

Did this cicada
mate before it died?
Sap-suckling from roots
for seventeen years
dark underground
to end in a mad burst:
mating, starvation, death.
Four days of sunlight,
of humming flight.

A cube of plastic
suspends a barnacle.
Darwin studied cirripeds
for over six years.
Strange creatures, upside-down
in their housing, legs propelling
food in and down to the mouth,
tiny volcano erupting
strands of flesh.
I leave this curl-footed crustacean
within six minutes.

v. Reptilia

Sea turtle skeleton –
my mind adds flesh and color
until it swims in Caribbean waters,
sharp-beaked stab crunching a shell,
sending clouds of sand
into shallow swells.

Hellbender salamander –
North American giant,
elusive occupant
of the Appalachian Trail –
now occupant of this jar,
belly slit, wrinkled, crummy,
rusty red, eyes folded
into skin above a wide-seamed mouth.
It waggled with a belly-dragging gait,
flat tongue flicking out.

vi. Aves

Wooden board, pegged-down legs:
nine, each different, not paired,

claws curved, gripping wood,
a scaly leg ending in air,

an entire body amputated –
stumps that stop, dusty glue and cobwebs,

hawk foot –
mouse trembling, claws grasping –

duck foot –
paddling through pond weeds –

sparrow foot –
rustling delicate branches, seeds.

VIII. Mammalia, Monotremata

The platypus, two feet long,
tip of beak to end of tail,
head taxidermied upwards,
squints, smiles, beak line curving up,
fur thick, insulating,
rubbery beak dried hard in death.

Alive, the sensitive beak
sees electricity;
the platypus hunts underwater,
eyes tightly closed,
looking for pulses –
crayfish heartbeats,
skittering insect larvae –
food can stay still,
but it can't switch off.

Blind, eyes covered
with a pink skin layer,
young platypus squirm
in deep dark, safe and blue
with heat from mother
who squeezes out thick cream
to pool in her fur.

Once called "paradoxus,"
it was thought a hoax,
the specimens were searched
for stitches attaching duck-like beak
to beaver-like body.
But it lives, even now, in Australia,
rummaging leaves in streambeds,
snatching edibles, head swishing
back and forth, eyes squeezed shut,
feeling rocks, logs, leaves,
drawing maps of riverbeds.

ix. Mammalia, Homo sapiens

Shells, jars, humming silence.

I respirate in this room
of expired respiration.

The eurypterid,
pale swathes on stone,
hunted the seas
millions of years ago,
left an impression.

Particles the heron inhaled
in life were particles
the eurypterid excreted,
particles that evaporated,
that rained, that I now inhale
with each inspiration.

Illumination of an Empty Room

I hold the pink fetus
of the kitten
on my blue latex-gloved hand.

I stare at the tiny dead thing,
crescent-shaped and naked, with beginnings,
minute forms, of arms, ears –
small, dark, unopened eyes.

We cut open the mother,
her uterine tube
thickly lumped with a litter of six,
each ball packed with blood vessels.
We felt around the clotted walls
to pull out the frozen life on a string.

Now, in the sterile room,
cloaked in heavy formaldehyde
that sticks in the back of my throat
so every breath tastes of death –

here, holding the stiff, heavy cat in the sink,
rinsing out her viscera,
brown blood flowing
into steel wash basin;

after the crunch of cutting open
the ribs with scissors,
pushing fibrous muscle to the side –

here and now I believe
in Science, and Death.

I hold the cashew embryo,
feel the weightlessness
on the pad of my little finger,
stroke its tiny, soft, pink-skinned head.

I am full of empty understanding,
numb, choking, with grit
of chemical fumes in my hair;
alone, a poet in a room full of scientists.

Later, the hottest shower I can stand
washes the smell away.
Still, with every breath – I taste it,
and wonder what the chemicals I breathe
preserve in me.

A Smoke at Dusk

The night we sat outside
on a warm autumn evening,
friends, roommates,
you taught me how to puff
and taste without choking,
two twenty-year-old girls
sitting on a porch
in white rocking chairs,
smoking cigars
like two old men.

I thought the sky was filled
with bats, small pointed shapes
flitting, diving, flowing in flocks
over rooftops, darting
through the evening air,
but they were chimney swifts,
swarming to their brick abodes
at dusk, flocking to sleep,
riding in waves of pointed clouds,
twenty and more birds,
beyond the warm clouds
of cigar smoke.

The Smells of Good Death and Bad Death

We know why we can't stand
the smell of dead flesh.

My hair smells
like liquid chemicals
filling skinless dead cats
we scrape in lab,
their still-furred faces
twisted into squinched eyes,
their stiff tongues jutting past fangs.
This one was a Siamese,
this one a tabby,
you can tell how fat it was
by how many yellow globs
need cutting to see muscle striation:
pectoralis major, minor.

This cat under my scalpel –
too big for the shiny silver tray,
furred paw dripping preservative
onto the tabletop –this cat is here
because someone did not take him home,
while my cat, ancient, black-and-white,
mean as hell, is not dripping on the lab table
under the wrinkle-nosed gazes
of safety-goggled students,
because we kept her, even when Mom said *no*.
This cat, the dead one, stiff and pumped with fluid,
smells like inquiry and plastic bags,
science and mass-gassed death,
the dead-end of evolving genes.

But losing its last *oomph* of green,
the gingko leaf smells like moist earth
and autumn, like hibernation;
it feels like silk and rubber,
a wide fan with mountain peaks
rolling smoothly along its edge,
ridged veins, a sunburst of parallel lines,
leaf-braille: *this is gingko*, my fingers say.

We toss great handfuls of yellow
gingko leaves into the air, at each other;
they rain into the back of my shirt, stick in my hair.
The tree has exploded its gold
upon the red brick sidewalk; we scoop and whisk
handfuls and handfuls of the green-gold medallions
at each other, never too old to play.

And why do we love the smell of fall,
of thousands of leaves, dying and dead?

A Fall Evening

Standing at the pond's edge
I think of Ophelia,
of letting sleep take over,
returning to the womb.

The numb sea
reclaims countless children
and all ponds run to the ocean.
What is one more child?

I want to take the flowers from you,
your way of saying "I'm sorry,"
and put them in my hair,
dance into the water, but

we no longer know what kind
of flowers they are.
We have forgotten
what they mean.

Lovely Mollusk

Upon my collarbone
rests half a bivalve
no bigger than my thumbnail,
smooth, white.

From a beach of shells
in Northern Ireland
I selected this one,
with a perfect tiny hole
at the top; put a blue string
through it, better than any necklace
I could have bought.

A tiny creature used to live inside
with muscles, gills, blood, mouth –
all tossed and tumbled ashore
where, after days, or months, or years
I happened to pick it
from a thousand other shells.

What little bivalve
is better remembered
not just for the nacreous layer,
smooth, white, but for the tiny
animal once living within?

Feeding the Corn Snake

Flicking her red switch of tongue, searching
for the thawed mice, black and glistening,
she unhinges her orange jaw in the hot red light.

Her eyes glow transparent pink
under the heat lamp as she turns,
metallic, wicked, ancestral,
to look at me through the glass.
Of course Eve was tempted.

She shed her first skin yesterday. It drapes
on the table, a pale trophy.

Taking a mouse head first, she plunges, mouth wide,
into its wet fur, its feet folding back as her muscles
ripple it in. A bead of blood rolls down
her belly, matching her scales.

Soon only the tail is left, but the light
shines through her, and I see the dark bulge sliding
to her thicker parts until it smoothes and is gone;
she lifts herself, turns her head, looks for more.

The Ninth Commandment

It wasn't the watching –
a film of chimps, a gang of them, hunting
a Colobus monkey. It wasn't the suspense
of the chase, blockers cutting off escape
routes, alpha male moving in, making
the kill. It wasn't the screaming fear
of the prey or the screaming excitement
of the predators, on-looking female chimps
on the ground, babies clutched to their bellies,
while the males scaled the trees
to surround the chosen one.

> It was the false witness borne,
> resonating in long-dead
> jeers and rotten fruit thrown
> at neighbors twitching on a spike,
> or a spit, or the gallows, or a tree branch –

trembling through excitement
in even the narrator's voice,
and in me, seeing myself up there
in those trees, canines gleaming
warm with marrow and flesh.

Thermodynamics of Immortality

When I die, scatter my ashes to the wind to settle
on a forest floor where earthworms buffet

through rich humus, where I pass from intestines
as nutrients taken by acorns, sprout, stretch

toward sunlight, year after year, inch my way to a branch
steeped with cicada eggs so I fall to the ground

and burrow, eat sap for seventeen years,
burst forth for two frenzied days seeking a mate,

when a burnt-ember cardinal snatches me, red
and cackling, catching warm air pockets from the pavement

until winter moves in; I huddle on a branch, fall asleep,
thud to the cold ground, dissolve slowly

into the icy creek, flow like mercury,
weave over stones around roots under branches, turn warm,

briny, pull into a spiny starfish, pump
into slow feet, and crawl again.

IV. Descent

Pure Admiration

In the belly of the cave
where perfect dark hangs its cloak,
where gossamer threads drape over stone,
where great pinnacles clear as ice grow
by trickle and drip of mineral
carried by water through miles
of jigsaw cracks,

they come, wriggling
through water-widened crevasses,
guttural sounds echoing in the slick
cathedral halls of stone;
they come, sliding, grasping,
sloshing and rustling through water
still winding through the solid,
the changing, rock.

With thick insulating skins, ropy
appendages, waterlogged feet,
waists cinched metallic,
heavy, hard protection
at their heads. With lamps.
They are the first and only
to admire the rock.

The instant the beam hits,
the crystals begin to turn, slowly,
opaque white, muddied
at the first soft touch of light.

Mating of the Silkworm Moth

His quill-feather antennae twitch
with her effervesce of a single particle,

inscribing a message onto his nerves,
launching him into the velvet dark

where he follows barely perceptible
breadcrumbs of chemical breath,

tracing her perfume until it thickens
in the ink of night, until she

permeates his senses, her pheromones
swelling in the air, solidifying

into herself, there, on a leaf
in the dark, where he finds her.

The Lake District

Sometimes we come upon a carcass.
Once I found a ram's skull,
rippling horns curving away
from huge holes once filled with eyes.
Once, just a sweep of wool,
dirty, bloodied, smeared across the grass
and into mud. I wondered
what predators hid in these steep hills –
Sheepdogs gone bad?
Large birds, beaked to sever vertebrae
at the base of the skull?
What predators other than gravity?

We walk in springtime
when mothers call:
A low, gravelly BAA from the ewes – *stay close.*
A high-pitched *baa!* from the lambs, who stumble,
blinded beneath the thick fern cover of hillsides.
We hear panic in both voices
until they find each other and fall quiet.

Sometimes we hear a little one call,
call, and call,
and we follow the winding trail
beaten out by thin hooves over seasons,
stop for a drink of water,
fix a shoelace, crest the hill,
and still we hear it calling.

Plumed Magician

We think we spy
through binocular
lenses,

but this small
white-and-brown
plumed falcon
sits in high treetops,
ignoring us,

escaping us.

*

How many days
do we walk,
searching the skies
for her dart-shaped
shadow, while

she watches
a thread
on my coat
unravel.

*

Today in the park
we glimpse her

flitting from bare
white birch bark
to dense cluster
of green pine.

Then our Merlin
simply disappears.

Fallen Armor

When my friend's brain burst a small secret
called *aneurism,* killing him,
I was glad he was not an only child.

We had two children, Mom said,
to replace your dad and me but not add
to the brimming human population.

After I was born, Dad got "fixed."
Later, happy to see Daddy home,
my brother took a running leap into his lap.

*

    With sea turtles, odds are stacked
    in favor of survival only if the mother
    successfully buries her clutch,

    if no ants attack a just-hatched egg,
    leaving a sunken leathery shell
    and tiny skeleton inside,

    if rooting pigs don't crush
    the buried nest, nosing
    the sand for a hatchling meal,

    if poachers don't dig up the nest,
    place the eggs in a bucket
    to sell at cheap bars for false virility,

if a hatchling wins the race
to the sea, missed by gull,
crab, fish, or eel,

if she completes the weeks-long
marathon to a swirling nursery of Sargasso
weed, a current pulling her since birth,

if she survives there for twenty years,
ventures into the open sea,
mates,

if she makes it back to her beach
and it is unobstructed by jetty,
still free of asphalt.

*

But there, poachers take her,
flip her on her back so she can only flap,
collect her newly-laid eggs,

rip off her shell.
It ends up here, bleaching
under a Mexican sun,

jig-sawed into puzzle pieces
which lock and sprout from the spine,
flatten, fuse into an oval,

while over and around, herbs
sprout from the shell,
grow pale green nerve cords,

veins, arteries of sage,
which some cultures use for prayer,
which I burned at my father's grave.

The Katydid Chorus

The katydid chorus rises,
metallic hum, answering, joining,
one by one until even the hum
of the plane above cannot be heard.

Safety in numbers:
when the katydid-hunter
strikes, the unfortunate victim
will be paralyzed,

a frozen snack for larvae to eat,
day by day, still fresh meat
until it expires: but the chorus
sounds no quieter.

We are connected,
for the katydid has made it as far,
and we share a spot
on its branch of time.

Monarch Sunset

One night in August the trees burn November.

The lighthouse spins its cyclops eye to the Atlantic.
The full moon rises ivory in the purple sky,
the sun tilts low on the horizon, sends
its swathe of light simmering across the bay.

But the conflagration is on the peninsula's trees:
hundreds of monarchs pairing tip to tip,
flecked with dying day,
melting green leaves with copper,
blazing with slow thermal radiance,
pausing on these trees, for this hour,
to gather and merge in flame.

Spherical Motion

There is movement in this sphere,
of millimeter-
measured subduction,
oceanic trenches widening,
sulphurous vents
bubbling gaseous fumes,
mountain ranges pushing above
the sea-line after earthquakes,
pulling calcium shells inland
to harden in the desert sun,
dry-cracking mud flats
stripped of water,
oxygen-silicon tetrahedra
crystallizing halite, quartz, talc,
coral reefs stacking pinhead
houses one upon another,
octagon-columned pathways
torn asunder,
edging the base of one country
and the tip of its neighbor,
magma pockets rising from deep
layers of rock,
bulging into batholiths, wrenching
into canyons –
four-and-a-half-billion years of rock
birthing and swallowing itself
in an unceasing groan.

There is movement on this sphere,
of floss-
spinning arthropods,
ungulate toes widening,
methane-venting fauna
leaking green fumes,
naked mole rats pushing soil
in blind trembling lines,
pulling roots to gnaw
with translucent teeth,
cackling shore birds
dancing across water,
chlorophyll in bud and leaf
sculpting stamen, pistil, petal
from sunlight, gold dusted
upon fuzz-legged bees
packing pollen into stacked
octagons of wax,
microscopic creatures
sucking tidbits within moss,
giant leather-backed reptiles
rising from deep ocean trenches,
bursting to the surface, wrenching
into air –
one-hundred-fifty years or less
will see each birthed and swallowed
in the unceasing groan.

v. Moult

Of Caddisflies and Kings

At Northbrook, for Dave

And then we tried the far bank,
along the lock, through the trees,
finding roots that would hold us
as we climbed down into the river,
and the water was clean, yet thick
with carapaces of thousands of caddisflies
which fluttered as thick in the air,
and we waded into the cold, flowing water,
late May, with these thousands, bursting
into a new element, a new relationship
to gravity – and we stood together
in the gentle current, as some
dropped their wings in the torrent,
never to pull from the river's meniscus,
and some lifted as mist, a brief,
many-legged breath –
a spider floated past on a raft of moss,
hailing us with its forelimbs, spinning off
into eddies unknown –
and the mayflies arabesqued in the lowering sun,
and this, we understood, was how,
each year, the river came to fly.

Chicken as time-piece

The wind knocks metallic at the mail slot,
and the sky lightens, by degrees –
                              ten degrees blue
on Humboldt's Cyanometer is morning here, where hens
peek through their metal window until we slide
the door open and they high-step down the gangplank,
onto their sea of farm lawn.
                    Twelve degrees blue and it's feeding time.
Fifteen and the truck comes down the lane. On the far side
of the wall comes lowing, cows, calling the truck for hay.

Fifteen degrees blue and we will have eggs from yesterday,
twenty degrees means today's are laid: warm, clean, brown.
                                                    The hens
follow us across the yard, chuckling. 'It is we who keep the time,
We put ourselves to bed, and you will listen.'

       Again, morning, and the degree of sky says, go –

Persephone

Who needs Ovid when you have
rescue hens? These girls
have never seen daylight; have
never stretched their wings (so
how can they understand
the purpose of wings?), have
never felt earth or known sundown.

Two days out, and the one I think
is writhing in death-throes is
dust-bathing, wriggling her naked,
feather-bare body into the dirt,
squeezing eyes shut with each ungainly
wag and roll. That a chicken can be plucked
and still alive shows man's failing.

          Now they have made it
from the dark, they will transform.

Ab ovo

The first egg she ever laid
was a constellation-perfect,
speckledy-brown, tight-cast-
sand-dunes, geologic-time
                        egg.

This petite pullets' egg is the most beautiful we've ever seen.
We will await her next with eager wonder.
                Or think: she couldn't possibly do so well again.

We will think it should taste particularly divine,
                or we will think that eating it may be a sin.

We will celebrate it in its moment,
                or we will wash it, blow the yolk out,
                            keep it as a fragile, sacred memorial.

The pullet, meanwhile, browses on leaf and worm,
murmurs quietly in the rain under tree-shade,
dust-bathes, eyes closed, in the sun.

Pasture, 7am

The impression of a hare
is that of a 'Z'.
With the lower line always
in grassy imagination; the feet,
always hidden.

The impression of a hare
is that of a small dog
in a green sea, larger
than you would expect;
a burst of potential energy.

The impression of a hare
is of the singular,
then plural,
then once more singular,
as it turns its head.

The impression of a hare
of one of advancement,
despite the definite lope
of the fact
moving away.

Criatura

Changes shape. Wears scales,
wears fur. Occasionally, claws:
        natural state, retracted.

Criatura wears marvellous dense pelt,
scent changes with tide –
fresh moss, ripe old apples, new hay.

Adores being pampered, brushed,
        nestling with mate,
            rutting four to six times per week.

Criatura wears bottlebrush raccoon tail,
plump and soft; prefers to burrow or swim.

Omnivorous: requires rich and varied diet.

Indoors, will gnaw window frames,
        claw carpets.

Some nights, criatura fly, stretch
wings
      from long muscles down spine,
       span wider than height:
         vellum, cobweb, translucent,
          fiddlehead furls
            beneath shoulder blades,
              silk whispers, catgut-strong.

From the Storm

Today is not for swimming.

It is for
        watching the breakers,

            for laying
                seaweed laurels, for hoping

                        these foaming tentacles of sea

will remain within the margins

                we have invented for them.

How Myth Works

So that, opening the −30° deep-freeze
in the Museum of Natural History, revealing

the huge, coiled python skin,
           rolled
                    like a disturbing carpet,

          and moody,
     splayed feathers, a wing – a nightjar? –
                        half
      a capybara's coarse, sandy fur –

this likely Gryphon assembles
      (vaporous mist spilling
      with the heft of the lid)
all these ideas of preservation.

I recall the Gryphon of old
was known for this power: guarding
great treasure.
            And for this sadness:
mating for life, not taking another mate
if one died.

            In the mist I am reminded
of my mother's *nom de guerre*:
                    widow,
(how to remain a survivor might mean
      remaining unrecovered – but I trust

            one can heal and not forget)

and of our pasts, an assemblage
of all the static magic we rely on.

Kingfisher

We mine for words, panning, hunched
along the edge: they wink,
eye-motes. Most are malachite,
quartz, fools' gold.

What if the tips of our tongues
were prisms? What if the mouth
was a prism, refracting,
shot full of light?

Here – here!
Swallow this kingfisher.
It's small, but its brilliance will burn.

Terra nullis

But are the names ours?
                              It's a simple test –
did your tongue stumble on those pebble-vowels?
Or did they flow like water, like the murmuring tide.

Misquamicut, Watchaug, Ninigret, Napatree…

In the reign of Charles the First of England
Temperance Foster Perry oversaw the planting
of trees around the new house. Her sister-in-law
Elizabeth named the road Margin Street.

I've yet to understand how the family fared
with the Niantics, the Pequots, the Algonquins.

Though once, my father showed me a grainy
daguerreotype – a wedding photograph –
of great-great-grandfather Swain with a Mohegan.

              Where is that photo now?

On East Beach

I'm home. Watching the plover,
which is watching me.

Tiny needle of the tide-line,
stitching the hem of waves
to damp sand.

Choo-hoo, choo-hoo,
up-down, on the seam of the sea.

I'm home. Watching the plover,
which is watching me.

Harvest

The fire snaps in the hearth
        and geese call,
               passing low over the thatch.

It is the night of Harvest Moon, and dusk
is pink and orange.

A pale pumpkin ripens in the deep window.

                                      Beside it
                                      rests a grey hat,
                                      soft felted wool.

Glass tumblers of wine reflect

   slow smoke

                where
                         sage
                                burns,

                tucked
                in the hearth's glow.

Airing

The evening sky's colour: air
with light behind it.
                      What they
expected to measure when
weighing a body alive, and
                            just after.

This absence rouses worship,
expects nothing. We smell it
at early dawn, surprise snow.
Not blue, grey, purple or white,
it pretends them all.
                          Evening sky
the hard-polished metal
of a long-thumbed wedding band;
perhaps a flickering hint
towards the shy colour
                          of souls.

Fox Not Crow

I.

Crow's not returned because Crow never left.
He popped up on a detour, lent his feathers
to grief (setting aside some understandable exasperation
that Emily had it right the first time – it was *hope*, his little cousins,
hopping songbirds, that were the thing
but one could forgive the bereaved chap
needing a useful metaphor, and besides, Ted was also by-the-by,
this was about *him, Crow,*) and he'd never left.

Of course he'd been treated more loftily
by Edgar, rather enjoyed preening over the *nom de plume*
Raven, despite feeling huffy about being granted
a limited vocabulary.

I'm not just death and doom, no, I'm *symbolic of the omniscient,*
you see, Crow says, feeling Raven-y,
a swirling circling eye for *above, separate from, Godlike* etc.
Always here (because he never left,) but on high.

He clacks his beak shut,
shakes out huge feathers on rusting hinges.
And so a fine tempting symbol
for those who want to evoke *distant but melancholy grandeur,*
and of course *high-flown philosophical musings on death,*
me also being a carrion bird, though I'll have you know
I preferred organic long before it occurred to you lot.

Crow is now hunched, shoulders-high wings-tucked, on a bookcase. And so I am *both within and without, but, primarily, above.* No ground-scouring for me.

Which brings us to fox.

II.

Fox is
feet-a-feet feet
pit-pat
soft as
nose out
up
nose down

Fox is weathervane
she responds
barometrically
to the presence of spring
Fox hugs Earth
is Earth
moist musty freshrot green
Fox knows
roots berries seeds eggs
eggs eggs
young. Delicious damp tender
wibbly-legged bright-eyed

Sleepy mothers, worn out
tangy bloody mouthfuls

Fox sees things at ground level
watches earthworms rise
from damp grass
sees them wriggle-thrust or flash
away in a beak
SNAP

Feathers
bleah
so dry

nose in
dig dig dig
Earth holds
(worms aside)
den dark-safe
womb-quiet
soil-safe
Earth-quiet

rain as distant wash
circle circle wake
thorn-teeth
snuggle snuffle suckle
smallest paws
kneading

Refrain

When you see the fiddler
is he on the burning deck?

Or is it sinking, at an angle,

or upon a roof, in Rome,
and is it burning?

When you hear the fiddler
is the tune a tune of triumph,
or of yearning?

Is the fiddle playing
at precisely the wrong moment
when the fingers that are playing
should otherwise be saving,

reaching towards the fire,
or clinging to the deck?

And when you are the fiddler
will the playing be a saving
will the yearning be a triumph

can you stand upon the deck
with obstinate elocution
despite it sloping burning sinking

reach your notes across the rooftops
and keep playing?

Endnotes

The original text of *Darwin's Microscope* (sections 1-4) was first published in Great Britain in 2009 by Flambard Press.

Ex omnia conchis

'All from shells.' Darwin family motto written by Erasmus Darwin, based on his own theory of species transmutation.

'Darwin's Letter'

Italic from a letter by Darwin to J. Todd, 19 April 1882, now in the University of Kansas Library.

'Deprived of Its Medium'

Italics from 'Hope is the Thing with Feathers' by Emily Dickinson.

'Fossil Memories …or, what is left of Darwin'

Published in *Science* Vol 326 2 October 2009.

Acknowledgements

Darwin's Microscope was the outcome of my undergraduate degree in poetry, biology, and environmental studies. It is thanks to the support of my mother, my professors – Doug Shedd (biology), Laura-Gray Street, and Jim Peterson (Creative Writing), Karin Warren (Environmental Studies), and Heidi Kunz (Literature), and the College's creative writing secret society, Quill Drivers, that the manuscript came to be.

The book was first published in 2009 by Flambard Press, which was, in the words of the *Independent on Sunday* "one of the finest small publishers in the UK". They ran for 22 years until sadly closing in 2012. I'm grateful to Flambard for putting their faith in a freshly-immigrated, freshly-graduated, 24-year-old American whom they had never met!

Thanks to Flambard and the lovely first editions of *DM,* I set up a poetry residency at Cambridge University's Whipple Museum of the History of Science, and was invited to read at the Cambridge "Darwin 200" Festival, enjoying, with awe, champagne on the lawn of Trinity College while David Attenborough gave a speech celebrating the bicentenary of Darwin's birth in 1809 and the 150th anniversary of his magnum opus, *On the Origin of Species* (1859).

It was thanks to this early success that I felt equipped to pursue what has become another decade-long relationship: membership of the workshop group, the Nevada St Poets, to whom I am hugely indebted for edits on my subsequent poetry. To Mick D, Malene E, Sarah W, Lorraine M, Dominic M, David N, Jocelyn P, and Richard M: Thank you! And heartfelt thanks to my partner David L, who has been solidly supportive of my writing since we met.

When I stepped into the Oxford University Museum of Natural History in January 2016 to begin a year-long residency as one of their first three poets-in-residence, it felt like coming home. Along with John Barnie and Steven Matthews, and thanks to the support of John Holmes and the staff at the OUMNH (particularly Paul Smith, Ellena Smith, and Scott Billings) we had the time and space to write new work inspired by the museum's collections, history, research, and architecture. The resulting anthology, *Guests of Time*, includes Pre-Raphaelite and Victorian poetry as well as our poems.

During the residency, I met the incredibly talented artist Katherine Child, who also works to photograph and digitize the Museum collections, and she agreed to create the cover for this new edition, a "Kraken" pulling the title down into the depths – but the beast is an *Argonauta* or "paper nautilus," a tiny, seriously cute species of octopus. (Obscure cephalopod jokes are the best, of course.) Thank you, Katherine!

Several poems from *Guests of Time* and *Darwin's Microscope* comprise the lyrics for what is a significant step in my creative career: a song cycle. *Endless Forms Most Beautiful* was conceived by soprano Carola Darwin, who invited me to work with herself and acclaimed composer Cheryl Frances-Hoad. It is thanks to Carola and Cheryl, my excellent editor Jamie McGarry at Valley Press, and to Laura Ashby at the OUMNH, that we are able to simultaneously celebrate, as part of the 2019 Oxford Lieder Festival, the debut of this song cycle whose origins lie in the first edition of *Darwin's Microscope*, and the 10th anniversary volume you now hold in your hands.